EDITH MARTIN

SMART Team TOOL KIT for

Team Leads & Managers
of Recreational Facilities

The Rec Coach's™
SMART Team Tool Kit
by Edith Martin
Buddha Press
Copyright ©2021 Edith Martin

TheRecCoach.com
Buddha Press.com
Library and Archives Canada Cataloguing in Publications

Cover design by Kathrin Lake

ISBN 978-0-9948461-1-2

Table of Contents

How to Use this SMART Toolkit

If you have read The Rec Coach Leadership books by Edith Martin, especially, ***Lead with your Head***, you will recognize the acronym **SMART**:

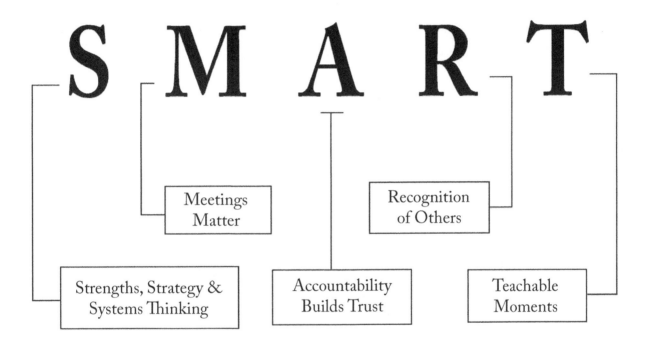

Each of these six areas are the keys to having a smart head for leadership and building teams.

The forms, exercises and pages in this tool kit are all proven tools for successful management and leadership. We have organized them according to SMART and each section has a brief introduction to remind you of the benefits. The table of contents will assist you to find the tools you may be looking for.

Strength Assessment Tools

Three Parts of the Mind

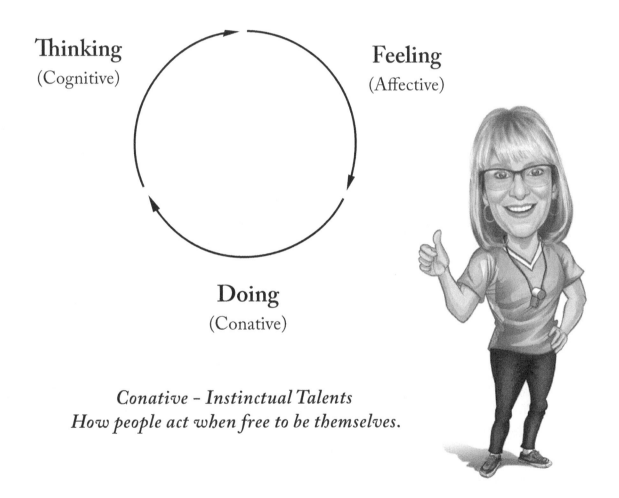

Thinking
(Cognitive)

Feeling
(Affective)

Doing
(Conative)

Conative – Instinctual Talents
How people act when free to be themselves.

Kolbe A Index Assessment

Kolbe A Assessment indicates your innate way of doing things and the result is called your MO (method of operation). It is the only validated **assessment** that measures a person's Conative strengths. It is used to gain greater understanding of your own human nature and begin the process of maximizing your potential.

The **Kolbe A Index** is an **assessment** that uncovers natural strengths and innate abilities. The most effective organizations around the world are using this tool to hire, retain, and organize highly effective teams.

Kolbe identifies four action or conative modes:

Fact Finder (instincts to specify, explain and simplify), how we gather and share information

Follow Thru (instincts to systematize, maintain and adapt), how we organize and design

Quick Start (instincts to innovate, modify and stabilize), how we deal with risk and uncertainty

Implementor (instincts to demonstrate, restore and envision), how we deal with space and tangibles

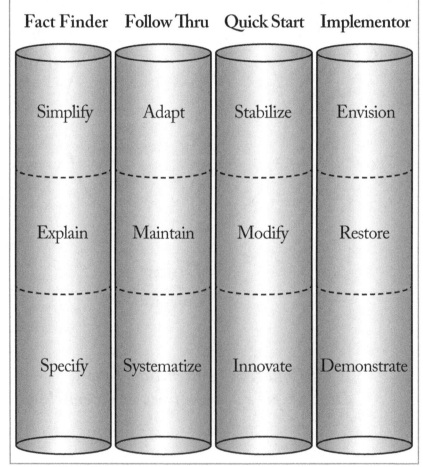

12 Kolbe Strenghts			
Fact Finder	Follow Thru	Quick Start	Implementor
Simplify	Adapt	Stabilize	Envision
Explain	Maintain	Modify	Restore
Specify	Systematize	Innovate	Demonstrate

Myers–Briggs Type Indicator (MBTI)

The **Myers–Briggs Type Indicator (MBTI)** is an introspective self-report questionnaire indicating differing psychological preferences in how people perceive the world and make decisions.

The four categories are Introversion/Extraversion, Sensing/Intuition, Thinking/Feeling, Judging/Perception.

Each person is said to have one preferred quality from each category, producing 16 unique types. Most of the research supporting the MBTI's validity has been produced by the Centre for Applications of Psychological Type, an organization run by the Myers-Briggs Foundation, and published in the Centre's own journal, the Journal of Psychological Type, raising questions of independence, bias, and conflict of interest.

The MBTI was constructed for normal populations and emphasizes the value of naturally occurring differences. "The underlying assumption of the MBTI is that we all have specific preferences in the way we construe our experiences, and these preferences underlie our interests, needs, values, and motivation."

DiSC Assessment

DiSC is a behaviour assessment tool, a quadrant behavioural model based on the behaviour of individuals in their environment or within a specific situation (otherwise known as environment). It therefore focuses on the styles and preferences of such behaviour. This tool is used to improve work productivity, teamwork, leadership, sales, and communication. **DiSC** measures your personality and behavioural style. It does not measure intelligence, aptitude, mental health or values.

There are four main personality dimensions or traits within the DiSC model:

Dominance: Describes the way you deal with problems, assert yourself and control situations.

Influence: Describes the way you deal with people, the way you communicate and relate to others.

Steadiness: Describes your temperament- patience, persistence and thoughtfulness.

Compliance: Describes how you approach and organize your activity, procedures and responsibilities.

Strengths Finder or CliftonStrengths

The CliftonStrengths Assessment is used to Discover & Develop Your Greatest Talents. It only takes 177 questions to uncover the one true you. But it takes commitment to become the best you. The CliftonStrengths assessment is used to unlock what you need to maximize your potential.

The assessment measures your talents, your natural patterns of thinking, feeling and behaving, and categorizes them into the 34 CliftonStrengths themes.

CliftonStrengths 34 Report shows you how to:
- Make the most of your strongest CliftonStrengths
- Understand your full CliftonStrengths profile and manage potential weaknesses

Utilizing Kolbe Assessments in Your Organization

Kolbe Assessments help to create a team environment where everyone is accepted, and people can be who they are. It helps team members to better understand how they are naturally wired to take action and also empowers people to do what they do well.

There are several Kolbe tools that are available to assist your team in building the best and most productive work environment.

The Kolbe A Index Assessment:

Participants complete a Kolbe A Index online answering 36 questions. The results are immediate and describe:
- How a person is naturally wired to get things done
- How a person successfully takes action
- What a person does naturally when striving to problem solve in their own way
- A person's conative strengths

The Kolbe B Index Assessment:

This is a great tool to assist you, as part of performance evaluation and performance conversations with team members.

Participants complete a Kolbe B assessment online answering 24 questions that measure how a person views the functional demands of his/her position. The result identifies which talents are a natural fit for the job and how the jobholder perceives the requirements for success in the role.

The individual's Kolbe A results are compared with the Kolbe B results to provide a report showing any areas causing strain and also provides information on how to cope with these situations.

The Kolbe C Index Assessment:

This assessment is very beneficial in the hiring process.

The supervisor/manager first gets clarity on the type of Kolbe MO that would be best for the candidate to be successful in the position. This is accomplished by using the Kolbe C Index assessment.

The Kolbe C assessment is also done online answering 24 questions that measure the supervisor or manager's functional expectations of a specific position. The results help identify how the Supervisor or Manager believes a particular job needs to be done in order to achieve success. These are the ways the jobholder is expected to take action regardless of the skills, intelligence or personality. One Kolbe C Index may be sufficient for a position that is the same and held by several people. The Kolbe C Index focuses on the position and not the person.

After screening applicants on knowledge, skills and experience, prior to applicants being interviewed, they complete their Kolbe A Assessment. Their results are compared to the Kolbe C on the position, and only suitable candidates would be interviewed.

Utilizing the Kolbe C in recruitment helps to get the right team members doing the right tasks for the greatest efficiency. Employees feel valued because of being able to use their unique abilities and have a greater sense of purpose.

When people are in jobs working against how they naturally take action, it leads to burnout, frustration and ultimately difficulty retaining good employees.

Organizations that are incorporating the Kolbe tools are experiencing greater employee retention and better team environments. They are able to make adjustments to ensure that they have the right people doing the right tasks.

RECREATION TEAM'S PURPOSE
(SAMPLE)

- Touch young people's lives, learning lifelong skills for maintaining their health, fitness and well being.
- Help seniors maintain fitness regimes that keep them healthy and out of the hospital.
- Provide a place for social interaction, sense of belonging and wellness for all community members.
- Create systems for the best customer service and facility maintenance that benefits all facility users.

When you create a plan, first, be clear on your organization's purpose and values.

Developing a Team Purpose Exercise

Creating a purpose statement reminds team members of the focus of their work and why the work is important. Job satisfaction and team members fulfillment comes from the inside out. For example, two team members who do the very same work, for one, it is just a job and for the other, their focus is wanting to make a difference in patrons' lives.

Hold a session with team members to create a purpose. Have everyone write answers to the following questions:

A. How do you describe where you work and what you do?

_____

_____

_____

B. Why does your recreation team exist and why do you do what you do?

_____

_____

_____

C. Who are our customers? Provide specific examples.

_____

_____

_____

Have team members share their answers, discuss and decide on the common ideas.

Distill this information into a few sentences or phrases that help to provide guidance, meaning and inspiration to team members daily, ultimately, why you do what you do..

14

Creating Team Values Exercise

Team values are the beliefs that are chosen to guide the team. They guide you in separating right from wrong in situations and helping to make better decisions.

Use the following steps:
   a) Have a discussion about personal values and share examples.
   b) Talk about the benefit to establishing team values.
   c) Ask each team member to write down 5 values from this chart, they believe would be the best for the team. Continue with the process on the next page.

Circle 5 values you consider to be the most important:

Honesty	Fairness	Efficiency
Initiative	Control	Competition
Creativity	Happiness	Integrity
Diversity	Peace	Respect
Learning	Cooperation	Teamwork
Recognition	Dependability	Trust
Friendship	Excellence	Hard Work
Quality	Success	Support
Commitment	Flexibility	Fun
Sincerity	Security	Safety
Innovation	Service	Relationships

* The values chosen are to be referred to on a regular basis to continually guide the team.

Creating Team Values Exercise Continued

Next Steps:

d) Ask each team member to partner with another member to collaborate on the best 5 values for the team. Allow 5-10 min.

e) Ask each pair to partner with another pair to collaborate on the best 5 values for the team. Allow 10-15 min.

f) Depending on the size of the group, have each group of 4 get together with another group of 4 to collaborate on the best 5 values for the team. Allow 15-20 min.

g) Ask each group of 8 to get together with another group of 8 to collaborate on the best 5 values for the team. By now, it will be pretty clear what the best 5 should be.

h) Next step is to define each of the 5 values, so team members are able to explain what they mean. The definition describes what team member's actions would look like living this value.

i) Final step is to decide on a priority order for the values from most important to less important. This is necessary for team members to know which value is the most important in a situation that comes up where two or more values conflict. You will know which action to take based on the value of higher priority.

Steps to Set Up a Strategic Plan

Planning provides a road map to show the team where they are going and how they will get there.

1. Start with a question such as:
   "If we were sitting here three years from today, what would have had to happen for you to feel great about what our team has been able to accomplish? Consider how your team works together, your customer needs, what is different, what challenges have been overcome, goals achieved, new initiatives started, your professional growth and development?"

2. Explain how to brainstorm with the group, all things are possible, there are no limitations. "Imagine you can do everything you can think of to be the best department at RidgeRock." Allow time for people to write their thoughts down or share their ideas aloud.

3. Next brainstorm is to get everything out the team considers to be their strengths and opportunities. "For Ridge Rock a **Strength** might be that we have so many activities to offer a diverse demographic of ages in our community. And an **Opportunity** might be how we can better communicate what each department does toward each demographic and see if there can be better coordination. This allows us to also consider how our strengths can be used to develop our areas of opportunities."

4. From the previous brainstorms, it is time to prioritize. "This is where we determine the goals to be accomplished, the resources needed, which ones take priority and then figure out what goals would be the focus in the first year, second and third years of your overall strategic plan."

5. The last steps would involve developing a draft plan, strategies and action steps to accomplish each goal for the first year. You may have 20 goals over the next three years. You can't leave this on one person's plate. "We need volunteers to commit to creating a draft for planning each of the goals and deciding on tasks to accomplish in the timelines." When volunteers step forward to draft parts

of the plan to accomplish each goal, they commit to share their progress and information with the rest of the team, to get feedback, before finalizing at the next meeting.

The plan can be finalized by another meeting or two when the rough drafts are shared ahead of time and people have time to read them and think of ideas that can make everyone's plan better.

Performance Feedback Systems

Employee Engagement:

Providing opportunities for feedback is so important to help team members feel engaged. A key factor in engaging team members is taking the time to check in with them and implement their ideas and suggestions for improvements.

There are a variety of ways to engage staff in giving and receiving feedback:

1. Offer opportunities for self evaluation and for team members to be involved in peer evaluation.
2. Implement reverse performance communication giving staff an opportunity to evaluate and provide feedback to their immediate supervisors.
3. Ask team members to provide feedback on changes in the work environment and to provide ideas and suggestions for improvements.
4. Ask team members to indicate what their supervisor could do to help them do their jobs more effectively.
5. Gather different ways to solicit feedback on how well the team is doing using customer evaluation forms, comment forms, surveys and having in person conversations. Other ways include monitoring the achievement of goals, whether worklists are getting completed and focusing on all the positive things that team members do.

All these strategies can provide some excellent information to let you know how engaged your team members really are.

Self-Appraisal Form

Name: _____ Job Title: _____

Dept./Div: _____ Supervisor: _____

Appraisal Period: ___/___/___ to ___/___/___

This form is designed for you to tell us how you're doing. It's your chance to step back from the day-to-day pressures of your job, and take an honest look at where you've been, where you are and where you want to go in your career. If you need more space, use additional pages (but don't feel you have to "write a book"). It's fine just to hit the high points here, and then discuss your comments in more depth with your supervisor during the face-to-face appraisal session.

The Elements of Your Job

Are you and your supervisor clear on performance expectations? What do you consider your primary responsibilities? Think in terms of the following: 1) What activities and results are expected from you? 2) What does your supervisor emphasize? 3) What do you spend most of your time and energy on? 4) What important things wouldn't get done if you weren't in the position?

_____

_____

_____

Your Major Contributions:

Where do you think you excelled during this appraisal period? Consider these questions. Did you: 1) Create a profit-generating/cost-saving breakthrough? 2) Solve a crucial problem? 3) Successfully implement a new idea? 4) Make an improvement in your department's work flow? 5) Complete a particularly tough project?

Progress On Your Previous Performance Improvement Plan:

What progress have you made on the areas identified in your last appraisal? Are you satisfied? What behaviour changes, new skills and achievements can you cite?

What Got In Your Way This Period?

How might you have sabotaged yourself? What's causing you ongoing problems? We're not looking for excuses, but legitimate performance difficulties – and suggestions for improving them. Also, how can we help you be more effective in general?

Where Do You Want Your Career To Go?

Where do you want to be in one year in terms or responsibility, management or specialist level and compensation? In three years? What must you do (i.e. improve skills, get special training, deliver results) to get there?

Confidential Feedback Form

Date: _____

Name (Optional): _____

You know better than we do how you can be happier, less hassled, and more productive. Now you can tell us, and remain anonymous if you'd like. Please take the time to fill this out and return it to us by (date). Hold nothing back: This is your golden opportunity to make (company or department) a better place to work.

The tasks I perform that seem to have little value:

_____

_____

Where I see duplication of effort:

_____

_____

The annoying or demanding rules/form/procedures I would eliminate:

_____

_____

If I were in charge of our department, I would change:

_____

_____

If I were head of our organization, I would change:

_____

_____

The best thing about working here is:

_____

_____

Reverse Performance Appraisal

Employees provide feedback to their Supervisors or Managers

Manager: _____ Dept.: _____

Employee: _____

Feedback Period From: _____ To: _____

	Excellent	Good	Fair	Poor
1. Quality of Work:	☐	☐	☐	☐

Thorough and accurate (requires same of others)

Specifically _____

	Excellent	Good	Fair	Poor
2. Initiative:	☐	☐	☐	☐

Takes action to improve department

Specifically _____

	Excellent	Good	Fair	Poor
3. Availability:	☐	☐	☐	☐

There when you need him/her

Specifically _____

	Excellent	Good	Fair	Poor
4. Planning:	☐	☐	☐	☐

Lets you know how/where department is going

Specifically _____

	Excellent	Good	Fair	Poor
5. Delegation Skills:	☐	☐	☐	☐

Gives clear instructions and builds responsibility

Specifically _____

	Excellent	Good	Fair	Poor
6. Relationships:	☐	☐	☐	☐

Mutual respect and regard for employees

Specifically _____

	Excellent	Good	Fair	Poor
7. Decision-Making:	☐	☐	☐	☐

Has, or gets, answers; doesn't waffle

Specifically _____

	Excellent	Good	Fair	Poor
8. Communication Skills:	☐	☐	☐	☐

Speaks/writes clearly and directly

Specifically _____

	Excellent	Good	Fair	Poor
9. Promptness:	☐	☐	☐	☐

Starts meetings, appointments, etc. on time

Specifically _____

	Excellent	Good	Fair	Poor
10. Time Management:	☐	☐	☐	☐

Completes work efficiently

Specifically _____

	Excellent	Good	Fair	Poor
11. Leadership Skills:	☐	☐	☐	☐

Inspires dedication and loyalty

Specifically _____

	Excellent	Good	Fair	Poor
12. Approachability:	☐	☐	☐	☐

Open and attentive to your concerns

Specifically _____

	Excellent	Good	Fair	Poor
13. Training/Development:	☐	☐	☐	☐

Helps with your professional growth

Specifically _____

	Excellent	Good	Fair	Poor
14. Creativity:	☐	☐	☐	☐

Has good ideas and solutions

Specifically _____

	Excellent	Good	Fair	Poor
15. Fairness:	☐	☐	☐	☐

Treats people with respect

Specifically _____

a) Team Building Questionnaire		Strongly Disagree	Disagree	Agree	Strongly Agree
1	Our team regularly reviews how well we are doing in order to identify ways of improving.	0	1	2	3
2	Team members are willing to 'lend a hand' when needed.	0	1	2	3
3	Our team has a clear and important role to play in the organization	0	1	2	3
4	Our team communicates openly. We don't talk behind each others' backs.	0	1	2	3
5	If there is a problem in the team, we generally leave it to the team leader to solve.	3	2	1	0
6	Our team has specific, measurable ways of knowing how well we are doing.	0	1	2	3
7	If anyone is not performing, it's the team leader's job to deal with it.	3	2	1	0
8	Our team treats mistakes as opportunities for learning how to avoid errors next time.	0	1	2	3
9	Our team members tend to stick to their own individual roles in the team.	3	2	1	0

		Strongly Disagree	Disagree	Agree	Strongly Agree
10	Team members feel uncomfortable giving each other positive feedback, encouragement and praise.	3	2	1	0
11	Our team regularly seeks feedback from customers.	0	1	2	3
12	Team members get upset when expected to do something different from their normal job.	3	2	1	0
13	Team members believe the team leader is the only person who can be 'the boss'.	3	2	1	0
14	If someone has made a mistake on our team, that person feels comfortable talking it over with others.	0	1	2	3
15	Team members regularly give the team leader positive and negative feedback, if necessary.	0	1	2	3

b) Team Building Scoring and Interpretation Sheet

1. In the boxes below, write the number you circled for each statement in the team building questionnaire. Then add the number of points scored for each column.

CLEAR ROLES & OBJECTIVES		MUTUAL SUPPORT		LEARNING FROM MISTAKES		SHARED LEADERSHIP		OPEN COMMUNICATION	
3		2		1		5		4	
6		9		8		7		10	
11		12		14		13		15	
TOTAL		TOTAL		TOTAL		TOTAL		TOTAL	

2. Mark each total on the wheel below then join the points.

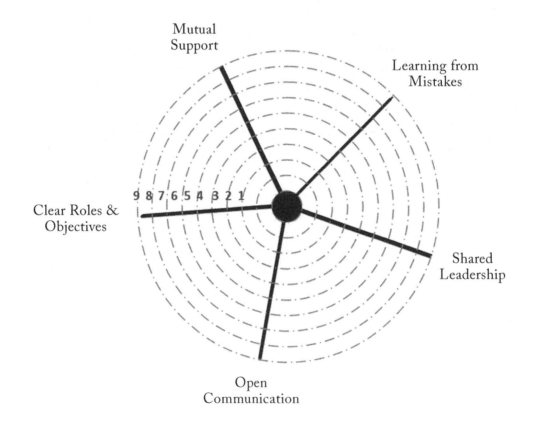

26

Example of completed wheel

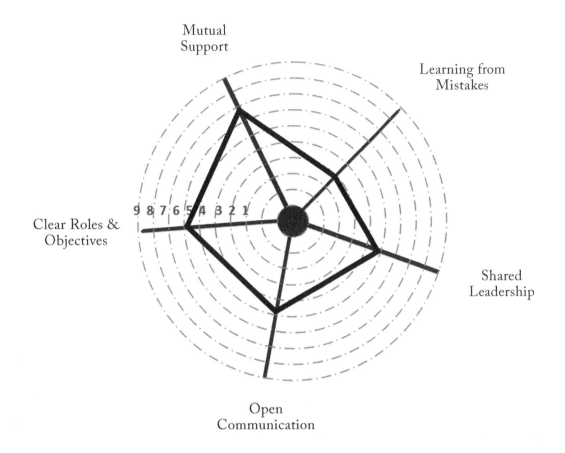

3. Add the five subtotals to arrive at a total score. Place an "X" at the position on the line below to mark the total score.

Your team needs significant team building.	Your team needs some team building.	Your team is functioning well.

c) Team Building Improvement Exercise

Given the scores in the previous exercise, describe how your team needs to improve in the areas of:

- Setting clear roles and objectives

_____

_____

_____

_____

- Demonstrating mutual support

_____

_____

_____

_____

- Learning from mistakes

_____

_____

_____

_____

- Sharing leadership

_____

_____

_____

- Practicing open communication

_____

_____

_____

Systems for Sharing Facility Space

Aquatic facilities have users sharing space in creative and efficient ways especially when the facility use increases.

Examples: While lane swimmers use the surface of the pool, other participants learn scuba diving skills on the bottom of the deep end of the pool. An aqua fit class is held in the shallow end of one half of the pool at the same time as a lifesaving class is using half the deep end while a small group of competitive swimmers train in the other half of the pool. Swim clubs use 5 lanes while other activities such as learn to swim programs are scheduled in the other 3 lanes.

All of your multi-use spaces in your recreational facilities have to be used creatively for maximum use and effectiveness.

For this we have some samples on the next pages.

SAMPLE LETTER: CONFIRMING FACILITY USE FOR A SWIM CLUB

RIDGE ROCK RECREATION CENTRE   44 Ridge Ave.

DATE: June 1st, 20 ___
Dolphin Swim Club
Attention: President Jake
Via email: _____ @gmail.com
Via email: office@swimclub.com

Dear _____

Schedule for September 20 ___ - June 20 ___

The following are the dates, times and your club space allocations for the 20 ___-
20 ___ season. This is based on your Pool and Meeting Rooms Allocation Request,
and considering the pool space and meeting room availability.

Pool Space in the 50 metre pool:
Rookie Camp Dates: _____   4:00 – 6:00 pm   6 Lanes

Regular schedule: Monday Date: _____ to Saturday Date: _____

Monday	4:00 - 5:30 pm	7 lanes (Lanes 1 – 7)
Monday	5:30 – 7:00 pm	4 lanes (Lanes 1 – 4)
Tuesday, Thursday	4:00 – 5:30 pm	7 lanes (Lanes 1 – 7)
Tuesday, Thursday	5:30 – 7:00 pm	4 lanes (Lanes 1 – 4)
Wednesday	4:00 – 7:00 pm	3 lanes (Lanes 1 – 3)
Wednesday	4:30 – 7:00 pm	1 lane (Lane 4)
Wednesday	4:30 – 5:30 pm	1 lane (Lane 5)
Friday	4:00 – 5:30 pm	6 lanes (Lanes 1 – 6)
Friday	5:30 – 6:30 pm	4 lanes (Lanes 1 – 4)
Saturdays	10:00 am - noon	6 lanes (Lanes 1 – 6)

Meeting Room Space:

Tuesday Date: _____ to Saturday Date: _____

Tuesday, Thursday	3:00-4:00pm
Saturdays	9:00am – 10:00am

Please note:

Club time is not scheduled on any Statutory Holiday due to facilities being available to the General Public: Thanksgiving Day, Remembrance Day, Family Day, Good Friday, Easter Monday, Victoria Day.

Please review the dates, and times, and advise me of any errors or omissions. I will provide confirmation of this 20__ - 20__ schedule and the License Agreement to you by _____ (date)

Current Rental Rates:

Effective _____ (date) the rental rates for the 50 metre pool will be $ _____ per lane per hour, and $_____ per hour for the entire competition pool.

The hourly meeting room rate will be $ _____ and the day rate will be $_____ . All rates listed are GST excluded. Rental rates are reviewed annually, and the City/Town staff will contact you if the rates increase.

If you have questions, want additional information or have any concerns, please feel free to contact me at Phone: _____ or email: _____ .

Thank you.

Sincerely,

Name

Position Title

Organization

Contact details

SAMPLE FACILITY USE LICENSE AGREEMENT

NOTE: This is only a sample. Be sure to check this language with your own legal expert.

The city/town of _____, hereby grants the Licensee, _____, a non-exclusive license to use, in accordance with the attached "Appendix A – Terms and Conditions", the following recreation area(s) or meeting room(s) during the noted time periods:

Recreation Area/

Meeting Room	Date(s)	Start Time	End Time	License Fee
See Booking Confirmation #	See Booking Confirmation #	See Booking Confirmation #	See Booking Confirmation #	See Booking Confirmation #

The Licensee is permitted to use the referenced recreation area(s) or meeting room(s) for the following purposes only:

_____

_____

_____

The duly authorized representative of the Licensee hereby acknowledges that he or she executes this Agreement on behalf of the Licensee thereby binding the Licensee to the terms of this Agreement (including, without limitation, the Terms and Conditions referenced in Appendix A).

The city/town and the Licensee hereby acknowledge and agree to comply with the terms of this Agreement which shall be deemed effective this _____ day of _____ , 20 _____

City/Town of: _____   Licensee: _____

Per: _____

_____   _____
Representative Signature   Representative Signature
Name: Name:
Address: Address:
Attn: Attn:
Ph: Ph:

Appendix A - Terms and Conditions

1. Definitions

For the purposes hereunder:

    i.   **"Agreement"** means this Facility Use License Agreement;

    ii. **"City/Town"** means the City/Town of _____

    iii. **"City/Town Council"** means the City/Town municipal Council;

    iv. **"Facility"** means any City/Town-owned building or outdoor area within which the Premises are situated;

    v.   **"Licensee"** means the licensed Party named hereunder, and includes that Party's members, servants, agents and contractors, as well as any Users (whether or not invited by the Licensee);

    vi. **"Parties"** means both the City/Town and the Licensee;

    vii. **"Party"** means either the City/Town or the Licensee, as applicable;

viii. **"Premises"** means the recreation area(s) or meeting room(s) specified hereunder and designated for use by the Licensee. "Premises" shall also include, where indicated by the City/Town, any corresponding player boxes, penalty boxes, dressing rooms, shower facilities and washrooms, coaches' rooms, and officials' rooms. If the City/Town permits the Licensee to charge admission to an event, for that event only, the "Premises" shall include any Facility lobby area, public seating area and ticket sale location as designated by the City/Town prior to that event. Unless stated otherwise, "Premises" shall not include concession areas, offices, mechanical and maintenance areas, and any other Facility areas to which access is restricted or prohibited by the City/Town for any reason; and

ix. **"User"** means any player/participant, coach or official using the Premises during the time allotted to the Licensee.

2. Additional Provisions

Any special or additional provisions that are intended by the Parties to operate notwithstanding any other provision of this Agreement shall be referenced under the attached Schedule A to this Appendix A.

3. Use Period

a. The Licensee may use the Premises during the times set out hereunder, and shall have access to the such other areas of the Facility as the City/Town permits for such periods of time as the City/Town determines is reasonable prior to and following the applicable Premises use period.

b. If the Licensee wishes to amend or cancel a scheduled use, the City/Town shall be notified no less than fourteen (14) days prior to the originally scheduled date/time. Fees applicable to that originally scheduled date/time will remain payable unless the City/Town receives that minimum required period of notice; however no such fees shall be payable if the City/Town is able to re-allocate that scheduled use.

4. License Fee / Other Payments

a. The Licensee shall be charged the license fee set out hereunder plus applicable and lawful taxes. If, in its sole discretion, the City/Town does not require payment up front and instead elects to issue invoices to the Licensee, License fees are payable thirty (30) days from date of invoice. Late payments shall bear interest at 18% per annum.

b. Where a license fee has not been specified above, the Licensee shall pay the applicable fee as established by City/Town Council (or its designate) from time to time. City/Town Council (or its designate) in its sole discretion may change fee rates at any time, and any new fee rate shall be effective upon thirty (30) days' notice to the Licensee.

c. Any deposit required by the City/Town shall be payable upon execution of this Agreement, and shall be forfeited by the Licensee if this Agreement is terminated in accordance with section 14 hereof.

d. Subject to section 3(b) of this Agreement, license fees shall remain payable notwithstanding the Licensee's failure to use the Premises during the times scheduled.

e. The Licensee shall pay all salaries, wages, commissions and fees due and owing to its employees, agents and contractors as well as all author's, publisher's and composer's fees and other royalties due and owing with respect to the Licensee's performances within the Facility.

5. Admission Fees / Concessions / Alcohol

Unless the City/Town expressly permits otherwise, the Licensee is prohibited from:

i. charging admission fees to Facility patrons;

ii. operating concessions within the Facility; and

iii. selling, distributing, or allowing the consumption of alcohol within the Premises.

6. Advertising

Except in accordance with the City/Town written permission, the Licensee shall not engage in or allow any advertising, promotional, marketing, retail or other similar activity within any Facility.

7. Rules and Regulations

a. The Licensee shall comply with all applicable directions, supplementary rules of use, regulations and laws imposed by any regulatory authority (including the City/Town) with respect to use of the Premises, and it will obtain at its own expense all requisite permits, licenses and approvals required in accordance with those applicable regulations and laws.

b. The provisions of Schedule A (Supplementary Provisions) to this Appendix A shall form a binding part of this Agreement and shall take precedence over contrary provisions of this Agreement.

8. Condition of Premises

a. The City/Town will maintain the Premises to a reasonable standard as described in its operating policies and procedures.

b. The Premises are licensed to the Licensee on an "as is" basis, however, the Licensee shall perform a visual check of the Premises prior to their use and shall report to the City/Town regarding any condition requiring maintenance or repair.

c. Prior to using any outdoor recreational field specified hereunder, the Licensee shall contact the City'/Town "bad weather phone line" to determine whether those Premises are available for use.

9. Clean-up / Damage / Theft

a. Prior to leaving the Premises after each use, the Licensee shall clean and restore the premises to its previous condition (subject to reasonable use wear and tear).

b. The City/Town shall repair, at the Licensee's sole expense, damage to any part of the Facility caused by the negligent acts or omissions of the Licensee, including (but not exclusive of) the Licensee's failure to consult or comply with directions furnished in conjunction with the City/Town "bad weather phone line".

c. The Licensee is responsible for safeguarding its own personal property, and under no circumstance shall the City/Town be responsible for any of the Licensee's lost, stolen or damaged personal property.

10. Spectators / Security

a. If the Licensee's activities draw spectators to the Premises, the Licensee

    i. shall ensure compliance with all applicable fire and building safety codes, and in particular, shall be responsible for observing the applicable occupancy limits as advised by the City/Town from time to time; and

    ii. shall be responsible for providing adequate security to ensure the safety of all Users and spectators and to prevent any damage to the applicable Facility.

b. Notwithstanding subsection (a), the City/Town reserves the right to, in its sole discretion:

    i. evict from any Facility anyone, including any User, who creates a disturbance or acts in an unsafe manner; and

    ii. employ additional security (at the Licensee's expense) for use during the Licensee's event if necessary for the safety of the patrons and the Facility.

11. Cancellation of Use

a. Notwithstanding any other provision hereunder, the City/Town, acting reasonably, may cancel scheduled times of use if:

    i. the Premises are required for a commercial event; or

    ii. the City/Town determines that the Premises are unsafe or unusable for any reason.

b. The City/Town shall provide the Licensee with as much notice of cancellation as is reasonable under the circumstances. Where cancellation occurs in conjunction with section 11(a)(i), the Licensee may expect to receive at least four (4) weeks' cancellation notice prior to the scheduled use.

c. Upon the Licensee's request, the City/Town shall make its best efforts to reschedule or relocate the Licensee's cancelled use. If the City/Town is not able to reschedule or relocate the Licensee's cancelled use, the City/Town shall forgive (or refund, if applicable) the fees payable hereunder pertaining to that cancelled use. The City/Town shall have no further obligation to compensate the Licensee (or any person claiming through the Licensee) with respect to the cancellation of scheduled times of use, and without limiting the generality of the foregoing, the City/Town shall not be liable for any lost profits or business opportunities arising from such cancellation.

12. Insurance

In its sole discretion, the City/Town may require that the Licensee place and maintain, in both its own name and in the name of the City/Town (as an additional insured) a policy of commercial general liability insurance in the amount of no less than $5,000,000 per occurrence pursuant to the Licensee's activities and obligations under this Agreement. Such policies shall apply as the primary insurance and not excess to any other insurance available to the City/Town and will include 30 days' written notice of cancellation or material change. Further, the Licensee shall be solely responsible for determining that it has sufficient and effective insurance coverage, acceptance or rejection of the same by the City/Town shall not in any way make the City/

Town liable to the Licensee or imply that the City/Town acts as a representative of the Licensee further to determining the sufficiency or effectiveness of coverage; the City/Town shall be provided with evidence of the requisite coverage prior to the Licensee's use of the Premises; the failure to provide evidence of valid and sufficient insurance coverage shall result in the cancellation of the Licensee's booking(s); and notwithstanding this section 12, the Licensee's obligation to place and maintain a policy of insurance covering activities relating to the subject matter of this Agreement applies only if the City/Town, in its sole discretion, determines that the said activities are not fully covered under another policy of insurance held by the Licensee.

13. Waiver / Indemnity

a. The City/Town retains the right to require that the Licensee obtain a liability waiver (in a form satisfactory to the City/Town) from each User prior to allowing User access to the Premises.

b. Notwithstanding any waiver form requirement, the Licensee accepts all personal injury and property damage risks associated with its activities on the Premises and the Licensee confirms and agrees that it shall indemnify and save harmless the City/Town against: any and all losses, damages, demands, claims, liabilities, costs and expenses of every kind and nature, including lawyer's fees (on a solicitor and own client basis) that are reasonably incurred in the prosecution, defense or appeal of any action related to the Licensee's use of the Premises; and any payment made in good faith in settlement of any claim arising out of, occasioned by, or in any way related to the Licensee's use of the Premises.

c. If the City/Town is required to take any action, incur any costs or expend any funds, howsoever arising in relation to the Licensee's purported performance or non-performance of this Agreement, the Licensee shall reimburse the City/Town for all costs it so incurs, including legal fees on a solicitor and own client basis.

d. This section 13 shall survive the termination or expiration of this Agreement.

14. Termination by City/Town

a. If the Licensee has breached or fails to comply with any material covenant contained in this Agreement, the CityTown may, at its discretion and without notice to the Licensee: suspend the Licensee's rights until such time as the breach or failure to comply is rectified; or terminate this Agreement and all corresponding rights of the Licensee.

b. If this Agreement is terminated or suspended in accordance with subsection (a), the City/Town shall be entitled to immediate payment of amounts payable hereunder (including interest) up to the time of such suspension or termination, together with any such expenses as the City/Town may reasonably incur in connection with such suspension or termination including, but not exclusive of, loss of profit or opportunity.

c. The City/Town in its sole discretion reserves the right to deny the Licensee any existing or future right to use City/Town facilities for any reason, which reasons may include the Licensee's failure to resolve overdue accounts payable hereunder (including interest) following the suspension, termination or lapse of this Agreement.

Notice

Any notice required by this Agreement shall be in writing and may be hand-delivered to the Parties' addresses as referenced above (or such other addresses as the Parties advise from time to time) or it may be sent by registered mail to the said addresses, in which case notice shall be deemed to be served five (5) days after depositing the same in any post office in _____
In the event of a postal service disruption, such notice shall be deemed effective five (5) days following the resumption of normal mail service.

16. Successors and Assigns

All assignees and sub-licensees shall be pre-approved by the City/Town. This Agreement shall be binding upon the Licensee as well as its successors and authorized assignees and sub-licensees.

17. Entire Agreement / Governing Law

This Agreement shall supersede and replace any and all prior agreements between the Parties respecting the matters set forth herein and shall constitute the entire Agreement between the Parties with respect to the said matters.

18. Modification and Waiver

No supplement, modification or amendment of this Agreement shall be binding unless executed in writing by the Parties. No waiver of any of the provisions of this Agreement shall be deemed or shall constitute a waiver of any other provisions, nor shall such waiver constitute a continuing waiver unless so confirmed in writing.

19. Governing Law

This Agreement shall be construed and enforced in accordance with the laws.

Tools for MEETINGS

Sharing Expectations of Team Members

This information can be shared with new team members and serve as a reminder to others at anytime:

- We all have something to learn
- We all have something to share
- We all have something to teach others
- Listening and learning to better understand each other is the key.
- Speak when you feel comfortable, taking responsibility for your own thoughts and feelings.
- Remember, people's opinions are not necessarily right or wrong. It is what they believe or perceive things to be. It is Ok to have a difference of opinion.

Interactive Activities

These can be used to start a meeting, work for both new teams and well established teams to focus on learning more about each other, about team member strengths, dealing with change, learning to problem solve together or see the value of others' input and help.

Circle Sharing Activity

Purpose is for participants to learn the preferences of team members.
Materials required, none.
Process includes:

- Participants sitting in a circle or around a table
- First person starts by saying something they like to do outside of work

- Second person then repeats what the first person said and says something that they would rather do
- Continue around the circle

Debrief the exercise by asking these questions:

1. Why is it important for us to learn something about our teammates beyond work?
2. How easy or difficult was it to share something about yourself?
3. What are the ways we can learn more about each other?

Variation

- Participants sitting in a circle or around a table
- First person starts by saying something they don't like to do at work
- Second person then repeats what the first person said and says what they don't like to do
- Continue around the circle

Debrief the exercise by asking these questions:

1. Why is it important for us to learn the preferences of our teammates?
2. How easy or difficult was it to share something you don't like to do & why?
3. What other ways can we learn more about each other at work?

Sharing Stories Activity

Purpose is for participants to learn more about each other and to trust each other a little more. Can have a work focus or personal focus.

Materials required: have coloured cards or candy for each participant to choose at the beginning.

Process includes:

- Each team member takes a coloured card or candy,

- Individuals speak when their color is mentioned and share what they are asked to share such as:

> **Blue** – an embarrassing moment at work
>
> **Green** – a time you made a silly error at work
>
> **Red** – a break through moment you had doing a task or project at work
>
> **Yellow** – a funny thing that happened at work
>
> **Black** – a scary experience for you at work
>
> **White** – an idea someone shared that really helped you at work
>
> **Pink** – a difficult task that you had to master at work
>
> **Purple** – a lesson learned and what you will do different next time at work
>
> **Orange** – a reason you are proud to be part of this team at work

Variation: Change what people share with a focus on their personal lives. Can use all the same information, deleting the words "at work".

Dealing with Change Activity

Purpose is for participants to reflect on major changes they have worked through, see that even though change seems to create problems, they can find ways to overcome them and be successful.

Materials: ensure everyone has paper and pen

Process: Ask participants to remember 5 major changes they have experienced in their life. They are to draw timelines of their lives and mark an X when each of the major changes occurred.

| Birth ——————— X ——————— X —— X ——————— X ——————— Today |
| 1994   2015 |

Participants partner with someone to share **one** of these major changes, only what is comfortable, answering four questions:

1. What made the change difficult?

2. What was the key to your success dealing with the change?

3. How did you feel before, during and after the change?

4. Refer to the time line and ask how the other changes going on around that time were affecting your ability to deal with this one

Debrief the exercise asking these questions:

1. How did you feel sharing these experiences with each other?

2. What did you learn from how your partner dealt with their major change?

3. What did you learn about the compounding effect of changes that are close to each other?

4. What implications does this have for us back on the job?

Variation:

Have team members share their experiences in teams of 3 or 4 This takes longer although allows them to hear and learn from more experiences than just one or two.

Sharing your Strengths Activity

Purpose is for participants to share with team members what their own strengths are.

Materials required: none.

Process:

- Participants partner with another team member.

- One partner will have three minutes to share what they are good at and have accomplished at work lately or over years etc.

- If the speaker says anything that diminishes or minimizes their accomplishment, the listener says "I object". The speaker must then retract their comment (i.e. "Ok scratch that") and continues.

- Other than that, the listener is not to speak at all.

- After 3 minutes, reverse roles, the other person shares their accomplishments.

Debrief the exercise asking these questions:

1. Which role was easier, being the speaker or the listener?

2. What did you learn about the person speaking?

3. What did you learn about how you feel about yourself?

4. How do you think this affects how you do your job?

Variation:

Have the participants answer the discussion questions in pairs rather than in the larger group.

Problem Solving Activity

Purpose is for participants to get help solving problems or get creative ideas for dealing with issues at work and also see the value of others' input and help.

Materials required: ensure everyone has paper and pen

Process:

- Each participant writes one problem or concern they currently face at the top of the page

- Everyone passes their paper to the person on their left

- Each person has 1 minute to read the problem or concern and write down some advice or ideas

- The paper gets passed onto the next person who does the same and this is repeated as long as time allows

• Return the paper to the original person

Debrief the exercise asking these questions:

1. How many got one or more ideas that will truly help them resolve their issue?

2. How did you feel having to give advice?

3. Why do we not ask each other for help more often?

4. What implications does this have for us when back on the job?

Variation:

Have participants sit in a circle. The first person explains their problem or concern and the others around the circle take turns offering some advice out loud.

The advice offered is only that and the person with the problem listens and thanks the person for the advice and does not go into why this idea will or won't work.

Use this same format to generate creative ideas for events and projects.

RidgeRock Rec Centre

Staff Meeting

Department:_____

Date: Feb 22, 2028   **Time:** 1:00 - 2:30   **Location:** Room 42

Attendees Names			Absentees:
Sharon T	Jane D	Foster G	Donald T
Rob B	Terry B	Joe D	Scarlett O
Darcy M			

1:00 pm	Welcome / Introduction / Recognition
1:05 pm	Warm-up Activity
1:10 pm	Review of Previous Action Items
1:15 pm	Project Updates
1:20 pm	Discussion or Topic 1
1:30 pm	Discussion or Topic 2
1:45 pm	Round Table
2:00 pm	Review of New Assignments
2:15 pm	New Action Items
	▪ Action Item
	▪ Action Item
	▪ Action Item
2:20 pm	Adjourn

NOTES:

Staff Meeting

Department:_____

Date: **Time:**   **Location:**

Attendees Names	Absentees:

Welcome / Introduction / Recognition

Warm-up Activity

Review of Previous Action Items

Project Updates

Discussion Topic 1

Discussion Topic 2

Round Table

Review of New Assignments

New Action Items
-
-
-

Adjourn

NOTES:

Org. Name:

Department:

STAFF MEETING AGENDA

Date: _____ Start Time: _____ End time: _____ Location: _____

In Attendance _____ Absent _____

Times

Welcome/Intro/Recognition

Review Last Action Items

1)

2)

3)

4)

5)

6)

Updates and new items to discuss

7)

8)

9)

10)

11)

12)

Adjournment

Notes

RidgeRock Rec Centre

Staff Meeting

Department:_____

Date: Feb 22, 2028   **Time:** 1:00 - 2:30   **Location:** Room 42

Attendees Names			**Absentees:**
Sharon T	Jane D	Foster G	Donald T
Rob B	Terry B	Joe D	Scarlett O
Darcy M			

1:00 pm	Welcome / Introduction / Recognition
1:05 pm	Warm-up Activity
1:10 pm	Review of Previous Action Items
1:15 pm	Project Updates
1:20 pm	Discussion or Topic 1
1:30 pm	Discussion or Topic 2
1:45 pm	Round Table
2:00 pm	Review of New Assignments
2:15 pm	New Action Items
	▪ Action Item
	▪ Action Item
	▪ Action Item
2:20 pm	Adjourn

NOTES:

Org. Name: _____

Department: _____ Date: _____

Meeting Notes

Items/Topics	Notes and New Action Items	Who Takes Action? Deadlines

Tips for Chairing a Meeting

- Your Job as chair is to facilitate. It is to keep the meeting and topics on track.

- When there is a guest or someone new that people don't yet know, start by going around the room, letting people introduce themselves and their role.

- Your job as chair may also be to ensure the agenda is circulated in advance and to book the meeting room.

- Delegate a timer to watch the time and let you know when we should be moving on according to the agenda.

- Delegate to someone to keep the formal notes or minutes (see sample doc) but everyone should also be making their own notes, especially their action items.

- Review the Rules of Engagement..

- You can keep things on track when a new topic arises by saying, "Let's park that for now," meaning you put it in on a separate list for future discussion when there is more time. This should be included in the formal meeting notes or minutes.

- If you don't already have a set policy, remind people to put phones away and on silent, only taking urgent calls outside the meeting room.

- Gently prompt people who have been quiet during discussions, to ask their take on the topic, ensuring all people get heard.

- Build into the agendas group interactions, games to accomplish tasks, brainstorms or interactive methods (see previous Interactive Activities for ideas).

- Review the actions items and who is doing what by when, before you adjourn.

- Set the next meeting date and time.

- Review the meeting: If the meeting did not go well (or did) use the feedback to figure out how to improve next time.

Rules of Engagement for Meetings

The first nine should be standard. Use the ones that work for your group and add your own as you improve your meetings.

1. Start and finish meetings on time

2. Be present and in the moment

3. Stay on topic

4. Respect each other's opinions and ideas

5. Listen when others speak, one voice at a time

6. Review the Rules of Engagement

7. Welcome all questions. Include topics in the formal meeting notes or minutes.

8. Have fun

9. Participate and contribute thoughts and ideas

10. Phones are turned off, unless there is an ongoing urgent situation. Those calls are taken outside the meeting room.

11. Laptops are used only for presentations, to read information on a topic, do a quick search or for the person responsible for taking meeting notes so participants are more attentive and in the present moment.

The Benefits of Rotating the Chair

- It strengthens everyone's leadership and facilitation skills

- It gives people a chance to respect the challenges of chairing a meeting

- Less likely that someone will be accused of dominating the team, including the manager, who may have to "let go" at times so people can learn

12 Questions to Ask to Improve a Meeting

1. Was the meeting needed?

2. Was the meeting beneficial, time well spent?

3. Was the agenda followed with meeting, starting and ending on time?

4. What progress was made on action planned at the previous meeting?

5. What could be done differently to improve the next meeting?

6. Were there items on the agenda that could have been discussed by email or phone ahead of time, so decision making could be done at the meeting?

7. Was everyone engaged and actively listening?

8. Did everyone have a chance to speak up?

9. Was there an element of fun and laughter, during the meeting?

10. Were participants clear on what action they are required to do prior to the next meeting?

11. Was there something on the agenda that provided participants to learn something new?

12. Do you need to have a way to open the meeting on a positive note or close the meeting on a high note? See ideas on the next pa

Ideas for Starting a Meeting in a Positive Way

Start each meeting with some round table sharing. Use a different question at each meeting. Team members can come up with others when they facilitate.

- What makes you proud to be a part of this team?
- What are you grateful for?
- What are you most happy about?
- What is the best thing that has happened to you in the last week?
- What do you really love to do?
- What would be a dream getaway or vacation for you?

Watch an inspirational Ted Talk to learn something new in the meeting. This adds a professional development component.

Show a youtube video that makes you laugh or shows something related to what you will be discussing in the meeting.

Ideas for Ending Meetings on a High Note

End each meeting with some round table sharing. Change it up each meeting.

- What inspired you at this meeting?
- What did you learn today?
- What project or task are you excited about?
- What will you focus on after leaving this meeting?
- What is one thing you want to learn more about?
- What are you looking forward to?

Team members take turns sharing an inspirational quote and what it means to them.

15 Questions for One-on-One Meeting Conversations

Choose a few to focus on each meeting and different ones each time depending on the current situation.

1. How have you been since we last talked?

2. What accomplishments are you most proud of?

3. What challenges did you face and how did you overcome them?

4. What are your current frustrations?

5. What would you say is your most important or significant contribution?

6. What are your goals for the years to come as you continue to work for this organization?

7. What are your hopes and dreams?

8. What specifically do you want to accomplish over the next year?

9. What do you see as the roadblocks or difficulties you might face?

10. What will you find most helpful to achieve your goals?

11. What kind of help do you need from me or others to realize your hopes and dreams?

12. What do you like the best about your job?

13. What would you like to change about your job?

14. What resources, knowledge and authority would help to do your best work?

15. What changes in procedures and communication would assist in doing your best work?

Tools for ACCOUNTABILITY

When you feel accountability may be an issue in your organization, even if it is only with a few individuals, it is often best to handle it in a group and let the group solve it.

Group Activities to Improve Accountability

Leading the Discussion of The Story About Everybody...

At a team meeting try this discussion exercise. On your meeting agenda this can be listed as Introduction followed by a Group Discussion. The Team leader reads the story below and asks for open discussion as shown on the next page.

"This is a story about four people named Everybody, Somebody, Anybody, and Nobody. There was an important job to be done and Everybody was asked to do it. Everybody was sure Somebody would do it. Anybody could have done it, but Nobody did it. Somebody got angry about that, because it was Everybody's job. Everybody thought Anybody could do it but Nobody realized that Everybody wouldn't do it. It ended up that Everybody blamed Somebody when Nobody did what Anybody could have done."

Author unknown

Team leader to read it twice. Use prompts for the discussion like:

- What is this story about?

- Where or when have you ever experienced this before?

- What are some ways to prevent this from happening?

- Are there specific issues or tasks that repeatedly come up where Everybody or Anybody should be handling it but it doesn't happen?

- Why does this happen? What can we do to change this?

- When something goes wrong and no one takes responsibility, there is a lot of finger pointing. What should we do instead?

NOTE:

Team leaders facilitating this discussion should look at who in the room has not said anything and ask them what they think about this story? How do they relate to it?

Leading the Egg Exercise

The facilitator provides the background; asks for four volunteers giving all of them separate instructions privately. She announces to the others watching that each of the four have been given a task that they need to be accountable for.

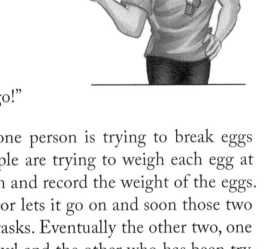

The facilitator introduces a number of props:

A dozen eggs

A food scale

A sheet of paper and pen

A bowl and a fry pan

Facilitator: "Okay, everyone is ready, let's go!"

Pretty quickly pandemonium ensues as one person is trying to break eggs and another is trying to stop them. Two people are trying to weigh each egg at the same time. One of them is trying to weigh and record the weight of the eggs. Those two seem to be competing. The facilitator lets it go on and soon those two start to cooperate realizing they have similar tasks. Eventually the other two, one who has been trying to break the eggs in a bowl and the other who has been trying to ensure the eggs have no cracks (and has almost given up), they too start to communicate, but still seem confused.

At this point the facilitator stops the exercise and reveals what the instructions were.

The instructions were:

Person 1 - Weigh each egg

Person 2 - Record the weight of each egg

Person 3 - Check all eggs and make sure they have no cracks

Person 4 - Prepare to make an omelet

Facilitator — "Were they each taking accountability for their tasks?"

Everyone agrees they were.

Facilitator — "So, what went wrong?"

Quickly the group comes up with all the things that are going wrong with this scenario. Some tasks go together like weighing and recording, but one instruction seems to duplicate the duty of another, while others are in direct opposition to each other like someone breaking eggs and another trying to ensure there are no cracks in the eggs. Finally, someone calls out they are doing things out of order. Someone else says there is no overriding goal or end game.

Facilitator — "All of these problems are true, and can be worked out through communication. Accountability in a group is only good if you are communicating the goals and considering how each task affects each other, and the desired outcome."

After this exercise the facilitator asks the question of the team:

Facilitator — "What is being assumed, misunderstood and/or causing dilemmas currently in your workplace?"

The answers may come slowly but start to compile a list on a flip chart of all the things that people feel are not working, or assumptions people are making.

Facilitator — "Can you see how each of us might be accountable for all or some of these things?"

Facilitator — "Can you see how communication can make a difference to these things?"

Facilitator — "Now who is ultimately accountable for the overall goals?"

Let them discuss, problem solve and decide what the accountability needs to be for these things, guiding them to the fact that while individuals may have tasks to accomplish, it is everyone's goal to communicate and ensure that the overall goals are met.

Your Personal Accountability Check

Accountability begins with you. Here is a list to reflect on, at the end of each day.

Ask yourself: Did I...

- ☐ Have a positive attitude
- ☐ Experience a teachable moment
- ☐ Help a coworker
- ☐ Add value and serve others
- ☐ Make excellent choices and decisions
- ☐ Take ownership
- ☐ Learn a valuable lesson
- ☐ Practice, if it is to be, it is up to me

Accountability to Your Team

- Help each other be right- not wrong.
- Look for ways to make new ideas work- not for reasons they won't.
- If in doubt –check it out! Don't make negative assumptions about each other.
- Help each other win and take pride in each others' victories.
- Speak positively about your team and your organization at every opportunity.
- Maintain a positive mental attitude no matter what the circumstances.
- Act with initiative and courage as if it all depends on you.
- Do everything with enthusiasm- it's contagious.
- Whatever you want- give it away.
- Don't lose faith- Never give up.
- Have Fun!!

Decisions for Accountability

Ask yourself...

- Is it the right thing to do?
- Is it ethical and legal?
- Do I have adequate training and knowledge?
- Would my supervisor support my actions?
- Is it something that I am willing to be accountable for?
- Is it consistent with our organization's values and policies?

If the answer is YES to all of these questions

Don't ask for permission, just do it!

63

Tools for RECOGNITION

There is nothing more important than regular praise and recognition. That means daily and personal recognition to each individual. Here are ideas of phrases you can use to recognize your staff. The best praise is customized for each praiseworthy moment.

Phrases for Praises

1. I am grateful you are on this team.
2. You keep learning and growing.
3. You have been so helpful. Thank you.
4. Thank you for your consistent effort.
5. Great effort. You make us all look good.
6. You are a champion.
7. I really admire your perseverance.
8. Your positive attitude lifts everyone's spirit.
9. I have great confidence in you.
10. I knew you could do it.
11. Your efforts are really making a difference.
12. You are a very valuable part of this team.
13. You contribute so much and it is appreciated.
14. Your accomplishments inspire the team.
15. Congratulations on an awesome job.
16. Wow, what an incredible accomplishment.
17. Impressive, you have mastered this new skill.
18. You keep improving. Well done.
19. Your customer service is sensational.
20. You are such a bonus to our organization.
21. You continue to delight customers.
22. You take such pride in your work.
23. Your opinions are valued.
24. I am glad you share your great ideas.

Recognition in a Group

The Clop

In a team meeting, instead of halfhearted applause as praise for the group or an individual, use a Clop instead. A Clop is one single clap created by the group. On the facilitator's count of three, one loud clap from the group ensures that everyone receives an enthusiastic audible recognition. On special occasions the group can actually provide a double Clop or even a triple Clop. This is usually enjoyable for even the most conservative participants.

The Green Card

Soccer uses cards to provide feedback about player behaviors in a game. For example: red card—banishment, yellow card—warning. We would like to introduce the green

"Way to Go" card

During a team meeting, or special larger meeting, participants can hold up the green card to signify Agreement or Way To Go! Encourage your participants to wave them spontaneously whenever they support an idea or wish to provide positive feedback. This strategy works well by allowing instant feedback without interrupting the flow of the presentation with applause, especially in large groups. When you are creating the cards, you might want to print a motto, mission statement, or a key message on one side.

The Team Medallion

Use a small object such as a special coin, medallion or stone to present to your team members thanking them for their contributions so far.

When the presentation is made, you provide team members with information on how the team member receiving the medallion has made a difference since joining the team, their strengths, their successes, breakthroughs and ideas that have helped make improvements in their position and/or for the team or the department.

Express your appreciation for their talents and what they bring to the team. When the medallion is presented you indicate "keep this medallion with you at all times and every time you see it, be reminded of how special and valuable you are to this team".

Notes to consider:

At some point throughout the year, each team member would receive this recognition.

The leader can involve team members who have received the recognition to provide information on other members who should be recognized as well.

The leader can collect information from all team members sharing from their perspective, what their peers could be recognized for.

Recognizing Your Team Members for Their Acts of Kindness

When you thought I wasn't looking, I saw you:

- Smile and make eye contact with every customer you came in contact with
- Go out of your way to open a door and hold it for a lineup of people coming to an event
- Pick up garbage while walking from the parking lot to the front entrance
- Leave a washroom cleaner than you found it, picking up the paper towel that missed the garbage can
- Help a senior walk out to their car when the sidewalk and roadway were icy
- Wipe up a spill you found in the staff room fridge
- Wash and put away dishes you didn't use
- Take work tools and other equipment back to where it belonged
- Clean up a big mess, even not knowing how it got there in the first place
- Complete extra tasks on the work list so all the jobs got finished

Recognizing Team Members for Taking a Teamwork Approach

When you thought I wasn't looking, I saw you:

- Ask a team mate if they needed some assistance

- Compliment your colleague on a job well done

- Offer a tip on how to do a task more efficiently

- Help to straighten up furniture and tools and put them back in place

- Collaborate with team members to solve a dilemma

- Put your best effort in to do your part on a team project

- Console a colleague who just dealt with a difficult patron

- Be the first person to offer covering an extra shift that needed to be filled

- Trade a work shift when a teammate had a family emergency

- Coaching a teammate struggling with an important procedure

- Stepping in to help answer questions when patrons are lined up waiting to pay to attend an event

Tools for TEACHABLE MOMENTS

Autobiography in Five Short Chapters
by Portia Nelson

Chapter One

I walk down the street.
There is a deep hole in the sidewalk.
I fall in.
I am lost....I am helpless.
It isn't my fault.
It takes forever to find my way out.

Chapter Two

I walk down the same street.
There is a deep hole in the sidewalk.
I pretend I don't see it.
I fall in again.
I can't believe I'm in the same place.
But it isn't my fault.
It still takes a long time to get out.

Chapter Three

I walk down the same street.
There is a deep hole in the sidewalk.
I see it is there.
I still fall in....it's a habit.....but,
my eyes are open.
I know where I am.
It is my fault.
I get out immediately.

Chapter Four

    I walk down the same street.

    There is a deep hole in the sidewalk.

    I walk around it.

Chapter Five

    I walk down another street.

Facilitation Tips:

Have your team members read over the information themselves.

Create a discussion by asking the following questions:

1. What thoughts do you have as a result of reading this?
2. What are the teachable moments shared?
3. What other lessons in your life come to mind as a result of our discussion?

Learning Agreements - Adding Value to the Team

Consider setting up learning agreements with your team members who are attending training in the form of a workshop, seminar or course outside your department or your organization.

The purpose of the agreement is to ensure the information is shared so it benefits both the individual learning and the rest of the team. The best way to ensure learning has occurred for the individual is for them to teach what they have learned to someone else.

This learning agreement is completed and presented to the person you report to when requesting to attend training. It shows your commitment to add value to others and help to enhance the team.

A Sample Learning Agreement includes:

1. Your Name: _____ Positon: _____

2. Description of the Workshop/ Seminar/Course/Special Training to attend:

_____

_____

_____

_____

3. Date, Time and Location of the Training _____

_____

Commitment to Share Information:

Following the training, I commit to doing a presentation sharing an overview of the concepts and aspects of what I learned as a result of attending this session. This will be done as soon as possible (i.e. in less than a month) following the completion of the session attended.

Your Signature _____ Supervisors Signature _____

Date Signed: _____ Date Signed: _____

Ideas and Topics for Inservice Training Sessions

1) Review Organizations Vision and Mission

2) Review Team Purpose and Values

3) Focus on Fitness and Strength activities

4) Practice rescue skills, emergency procedures and evacuation

5) Learn to use new equipment

6) Team building activities; icebreakers to get to know each other

7) Have food, fun and fellowship

8) Review policies and procedures including updates and changes

9) Provide facility updates

10) Share what's new related to the facilities, staffing and schedules

11) Health and Safety updates

12) Review roles and responsibilities and expectations of teams

13) Share upcoming information on recertifications and training sessions

14) Include professional development on Leadership, Teamwork and Customer Service

15) Share names of good books and great movies

16) Share statistics on facility attendance and revenue, first aid treatments given etc.

17) Share interesting facts related to the staff and facilities

18) Include engaging quizzes or contests- Did you know? Past History?

19) Have guest speakers on special topics

20) Use music and relevant You Tube videos and Ted Talks

21) Share staff info: roles, responsibilities, special assignments and those moving on

22) Show appreciation for teamwork and successes

23) Info on looking ahead or what is coming (shutdown, work changes, special events)

24) Include stretch breaks, time for reflection, questions and answer sessions

25) Share inspirational quotes and points of interest

26) Encourage staff to get involved with community charity events

27) Involve team members to help organize and share their talent

28) Recognition of new, current and boomerang staff (those who have returned)

29) Special staff service awards, recognizing years of service (1, 3, 5, 10, 15, 20, and 25 years)

30) Recognition of staff birthdays, graduations and anniversaries

31) Share customer kudos and feedback for making improvements

32) Ask team members for teachable moments and suggestions for future sessions

Team Development Game - Teachable Moments

Objective: Teachable moments learning about team development

Use: For a team building session

How it Works:

1. Each team receives a stack of papers, a roll of masking tape and bag of reward items.

2. Teams have 10 minutes to discuss how they will build a tower that is tall, strong and beautiful. They are not allowed to touch any of the materials given to them until the building time.

3. Teams are given the signal to start the 15 minute building time.

4. When time is up, each team walks around the room to look at the towers other teams have built.

5. As a team you are to judge the other teams work on their towers' height, strength and beauty and decide how you are going to reward them.

6. The reward items are only for the other teams.

Time Required:

10 minutes for the planning discussion

15 minutes of building time

10 minutes of judging and rewarding time

20 minutes debriefing and team discussion

Facilitating the debriefing and team discussion:

The objective of the debriefing and discussion is to review how well your team worked together and what you learned about yourselves as team members.

As the leader, you ask each team to discuss these 5 questions. Allow about 15 minutes.

1. What did your team do well?

2. What could your team have done better?

3. Did you have a team leader? How were they chosen to lead?

4. What would you do differently if you were to play another game like this?

5. How did you feel about having to judge the other's towers and distribute the rewards?

As an entire group have each team share their best teachable moments for them.

The Rec Coach Series

  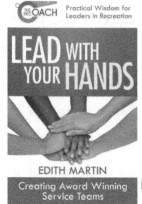 

The Rec Coach, Series for Team Leaders and Managers, by Edith Martin

*If you enjoyed this or any of The Rec Coach book series
please review them on Amazon!*

The Rec Coach's Lead with Your Heart:
Developing and Leading Teams That Care
Learn five basic principles that will enhance your leadership skills and help you develop teams of people who care.

The Rec Coach's Lead with Your Head:
Building SMART Teams
Learn five SMART teamwork strategies for transforming your team and your organization.

The Rec Coach's Lead with Your Hands:
Creating Award-winning Customer Service Teams
Learn five important keys for a leader wanting to create a team with a genuine focus on award-winning customer service.

Who is THE REC COACH?
ABOUT THE AUTHOR

Edith Martin is a teacher, author and coach with HR Management, and is a Past President and Honorary Life Member of the Alberta Association of Recreation Facility Personnel. Edith Martin is now the "The Rec Coach," inspiring others by speaking, writing and facilitating.

She is a seasoned, certified Kolbe facilitator, provides leadership mentoring, team building, customer service training, and assists organizations of all kinds with strategic planning.

Edith continues to be a lifelong learner, a dedicated member of Rotary International and is intentional about giving her best and doing good in the world.

To contact Edith Martin:
Email: edith@thereccoach.com
www.thereccoach.com

Available for consultations, mentorship, speaking and facilitation.